WHERE IN THE WORLD KONEKO CAT?

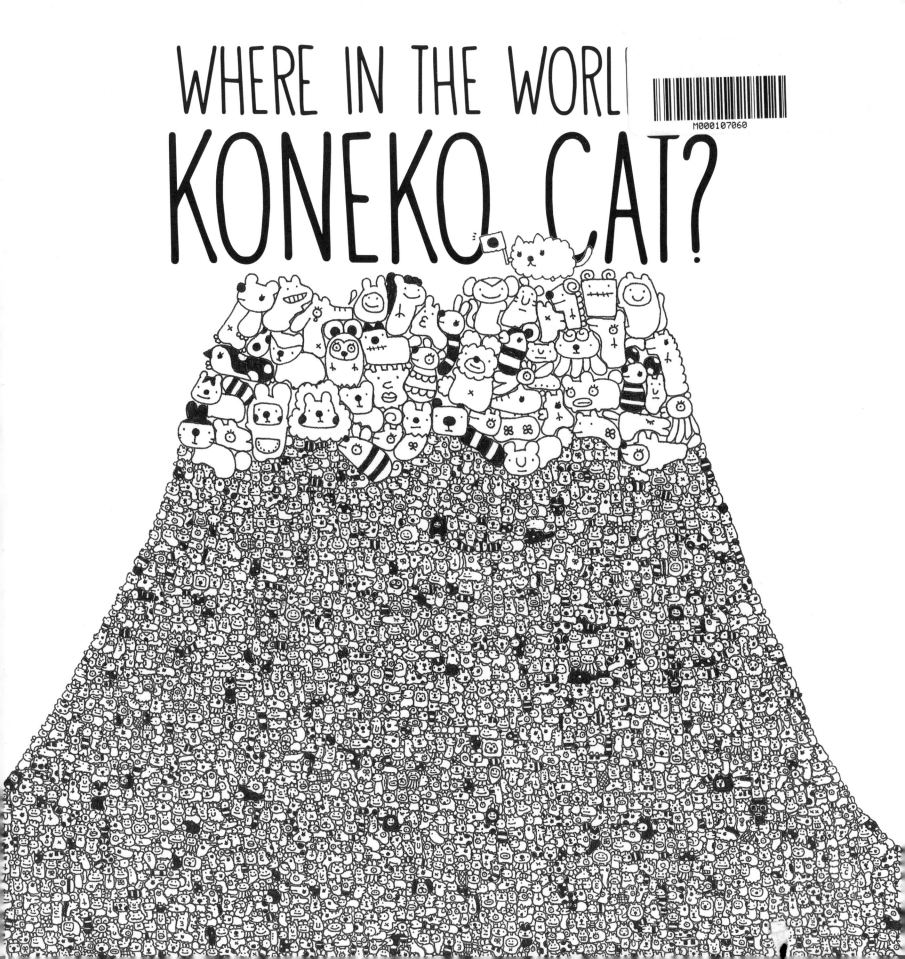

BALLPOINT DRAWINGS BY ASUKA SATOW

WHERE IN THE WORLD IS KONEKO CAT?

Andrews McMeel
Publishing®

Kansas City • Sydney • London

A SEEK & FIND ADVENTURE COLORING BOOK WITH STICKER SHEET

ITINERARY

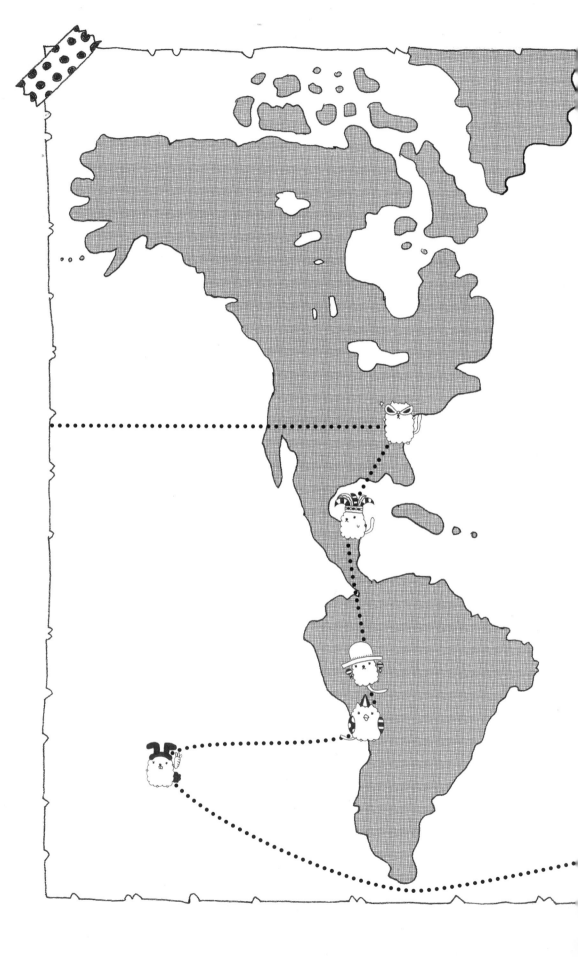

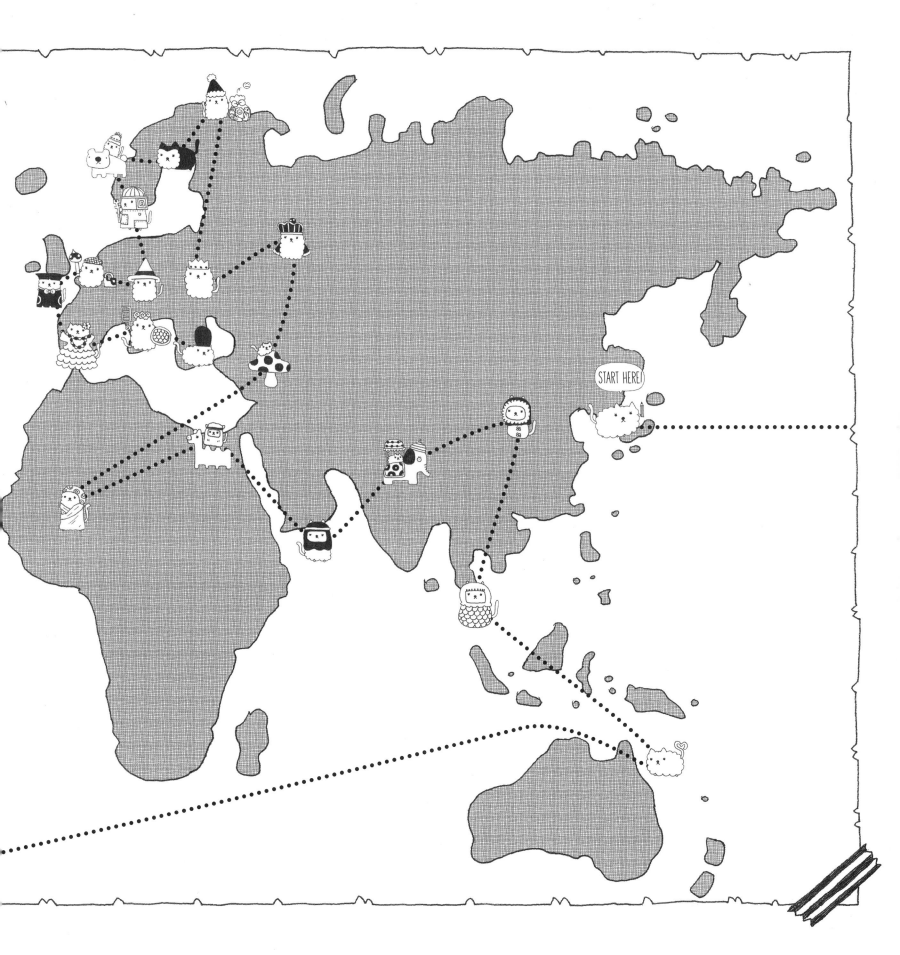

KONEKO CAT is ready for adventure.

She's off to see the **WORLD**!

1. First stop? The **U.S.A.**!
Koneko really likes New York
City, especially the Empire State
Building and the Statue of Liberty.

Find **KONEKO** and her friends:

2. Koneko is in **MEXICO**, making friends with fantastical creatures from Mayan mythology.

Find **KONEKO** and her friends:

3. Koneko is high in the Andes Mountains of **PERU**, hiking around the Incan ruins of Machu Picchu.

Find **KONEKO** and her friends:

4. Koneko is in the **NAZCA DESERT** viewing the Nazca Lines — hundreds of enormous animal figures that were carved into the ground in ancient times. This condor is as long as a 40-story building!

Find **KONEKO** and her friends:

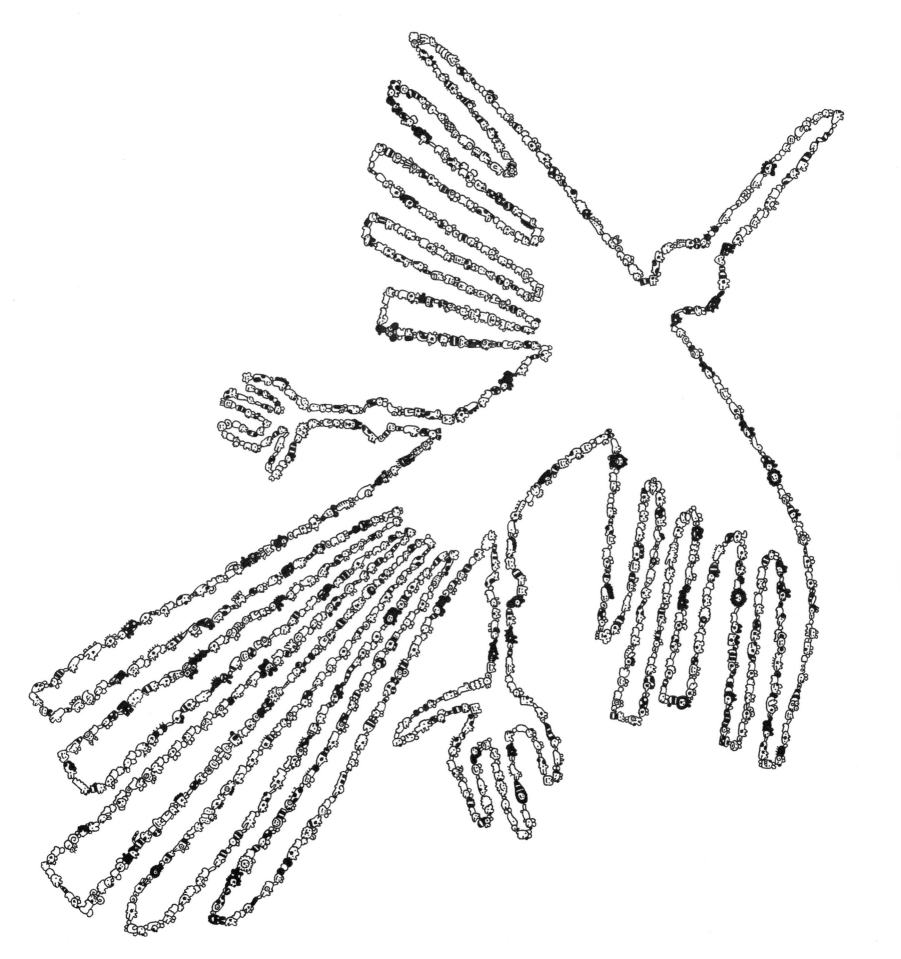

5. Koneko is on **EASTER ISLAND**, gazing at the moai head statues. They are gigantic!

Find **KONEKO** and her friends:

6. Koneko is at Heart Reef, part of **AUSTRALIA**'s Great Barrier Reef. It really is shaped like a heart!

Find **KONEKO** and her friends:

7. Koneko stops in **SINGAPORE** to see the Merlion fountain. It has the body of a fish and the head of a lion.

Find **KONEKO** and her friends:

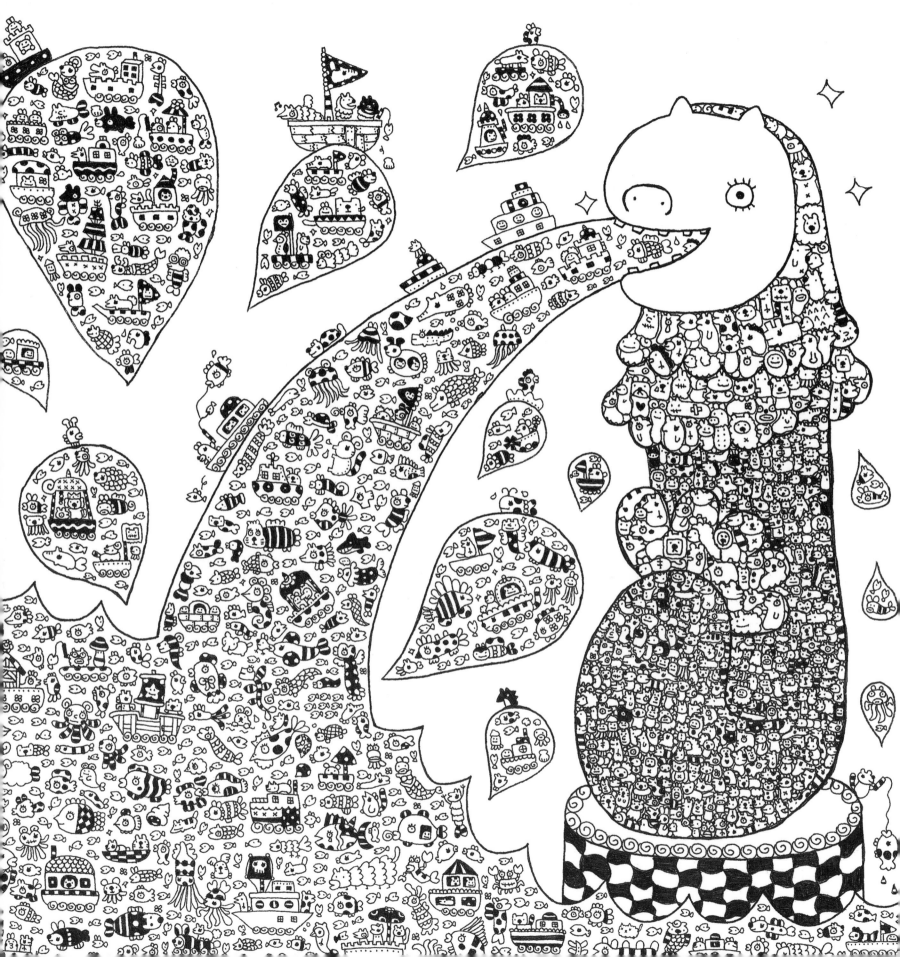

8. Koneko is visiting the Terracotta Army made for the first Emperor of **CHINA**. There are over 8,000 warriors, and every one is different!

Find **KONEKO** and her friends:

9. Koneko is at the Taj Mahal in **INDIA**, one of the most famous landmarks in the world. It is set in a large garden with a long reflecting pool.

Find **KONEKO** and her friends:

10. Koneko is on **SOCOTRA ISLAND**, whose unique plants are found nowhere else in the world. She likes the big umbrella tops of the dragon blood trees.

Find **KONEKO** and her friends:

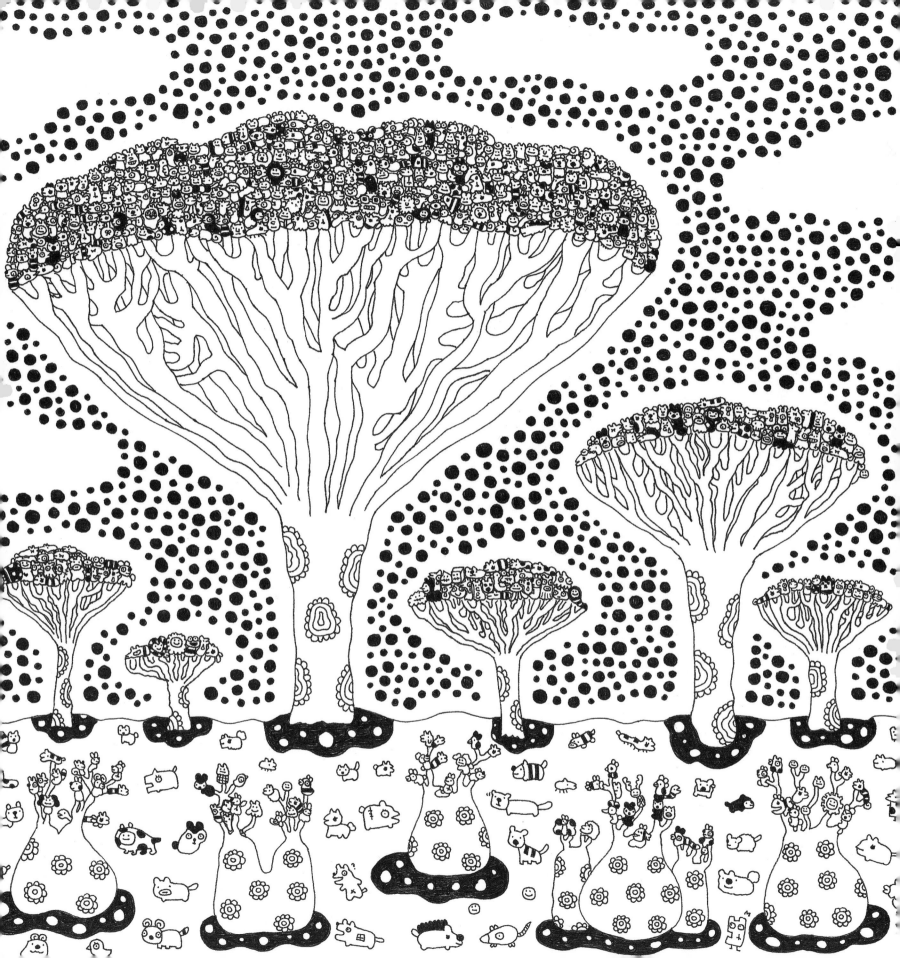

11. Koneko is in **EGYPT** at the Pyramids of Giza. They say the Sphinx is part lion and part human, but Koneko thinks it is one of her cat ancestors. What do you think?

Find **KONEKO** and her friends:

12. Koneko is in **MALI**, West Africa, at the Great Mosque of Djenné. The market in front is very busy.

Find **KONEKO** and her friends:

13. Koneko is in Cappadocia, **TURKEY.**
From hot air balloons, she and her
friends have wonderful views of the
mushroom-shaped limestone columns
where locals have carved their homes.

Find **KONEKO** and her friends:

14. Koneko is in **MOSCOW**'s Red Square, admiring the onion domes of St. Basil's Cathedral. They are very colorful!

Find **KONEKO** and her friends:

15. Koneko is in Budapest, **HUNGARY**. The Chain Bridge runs over the Danube River near the Royal Palace.

Find **KONEKO** and her friends:

16. Koneko travels north to the Arctic Circle in **FINLAND**, where she finds Santa Claus Village. The streets are full of presents!

Find **KONEKO** and her friends:

17. Koneko takes a short broom ride to Blåkulla Island in **SWEDEN**. Witches and their black cats hold a party there every spring.

Find **KONEKO** and her friends:

18. Koneko is in Northern **NORWAY**, Land of the Northern Lights. The bright colors of the aurora borealis dance across the sky all night long.

Find **KONEKO** and her friends:

19. Koneko stops in **DENMARK**, home of Lego, to visit Legoland. Everything is made of Lego blocks!

Find **KONEKO** and her friends:

20. Koneko travels all over
SWITZERLAND by train, past
mountains, cheese, and clocks.

Find **KONEKO** and her friends:

21. So many things to see in **PARIS**! Koneko likes Notre Dame and the Arc de Triomphe, but her favorite is the Eiffel Tower.

Find **KONEKO** and her friends:

22. Koneko climbs to the top of Mont Saint-Michel, on a granite island just off the northern coast of **FRANCE**.

Find **KONEKO** and her friends:

· ·

23. Koneko is at the magnificent Sagrada Família in Barcelona, the most popular monument in **SPAIN**.

Find **KONEKO** and her friends:

24. Koneko is in Rome, **ITALY**. The Colosseum is so big that the Arch of Constantine, just steps away, looks small.

Find **KONEKO** and her friends:

25. Koneko is in **GREECE**, exploring the island of Santorini. The hillsides of white houses with blue dome roofs are a peaceful sight.

Find **KONEKO** and her friends:

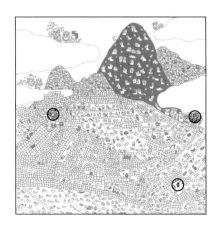
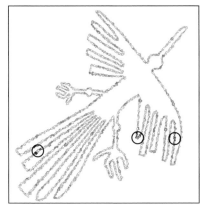
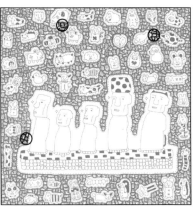

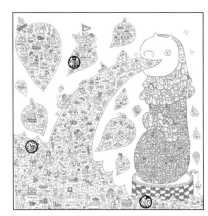
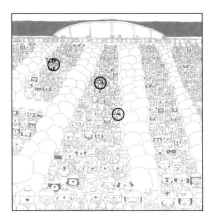

Tomorrow it is time for Koneko to begin her journey **HOME**.

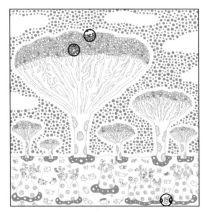
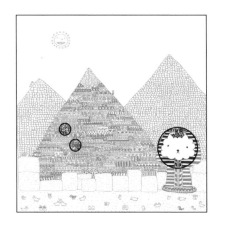
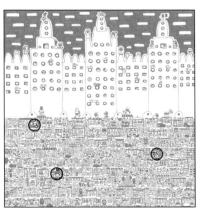

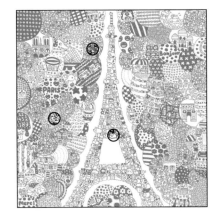

bye

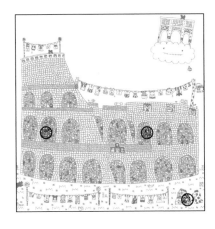
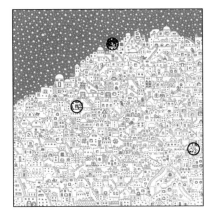

Andrews McMeel Publishing, LLC
an Andrews McMeel Universal company
1130 Walnut Street, Kansas City, Missouri 64106

www.andrewsmcmeel.com

15 16 17 18 19 TEN 10 9 8 7 6 5 4 3 2 1

ISBN: 978-1-4494-6622-0

Library of Congress Control Number: 2014946033

ATTENTION: SCHOOLS AND BUSINESSES
Andrews McMeel books are available at quantity discounts with bulk purchase for educational, business, or sales promotional use. For information, please e-mail the Andrews McMeel Publishing Special Sales Department: specialsales@amuniversal.com.